The Statue of Liberty

by Mary Firestone

illustrated by Matthew Skeens

PICTURE WINDOW BOOKS
Minneapolis, Minnesota

Special thanks to our advisers for their expertise:

Kevin Byrne, Ph.D., Professor of History
Gustavus Adolphus College

Susan Kesselring, M.A., Literacy Educator
Rosemount–Apple Valley–Eagan (Minnesota) School District

Editor: Jill Kalz
Designer: Nathan Gassman
Page Production: Tracy Kaehler and Ellen Schofield
Creative Director: Keith Griffin
Editorial Director: Carol Jones
The illustrations in this book were created digitally.
Photo credit: Shutterstock/James Kingman, 23

Picture Window Books
151 Good Counsel Drive
P.O. Box 669
Mankato, MN 56002-0669
877-845-8392
www.capstonepub.com

Library of Congress Cataloging-in-Publication Data
Firestone, Mary.
The Statue of Liberty / by Mary Firestone ; illustrated by Matthew Skeens.
p. cm. — (American symbols)
Includes bibliographical references and index.
ISBN: 978-1-4048-2216-0 (hardcover)
ISBN: 978-1-4048-2222-1 (paperback)
1. Statue of Liberty (New York, N.Y.)—Juvenile literature. 2. Statue of Liberty National
Monument (N.Y. and N.J.)—Juvenile literature. 3. New York (N.Y.)—Buildings,
structures, etc.—Juvenile literature. I. Skeens, Matthew. II. Title. III.
American symbols (Picture Window Books)
F128.64.L6 F57 2007
974.71—dc22
2006003376

Printed in the United States of America in Stevens Point, Wisconsin.
062011   006254

Table of Contents

My name is Jeanetta.
I'm a park ranger at Statue of Liberty National Park in New York City. The Statue of Liberty is an important symbol of freedom. Let me tell you her story.

A Gift from the French

Did you know that the Statue of Liberty was a gift from the people of France? They admired the Colonies' fight for freedom during the Revolutionary War. They wanted to honor the Declaration of Independence. The gift was France's way of saying, "Good job, America!"

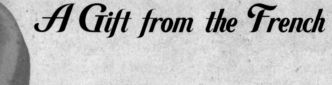

French soldiers and sailors fought side-by-side with American troops during the Revolutionary War. Together, they defeated the British and won the war.

Making the Statue

A French artist named Frederic-Auguste Bartholdi drew up plans for the Statue of Liberty in 1874.

Workers in France used copper sheets for the statue's outside surface, or skin. The sheets were about as thick as two pennies. Workers pounded the copper sheets onto wooden molds.

When the Statue of Liberty was first built, she was reddish brown—the color of new copper. Copper changes color when it's left outside. It turns light green or blue. This change in color is called oxidation.

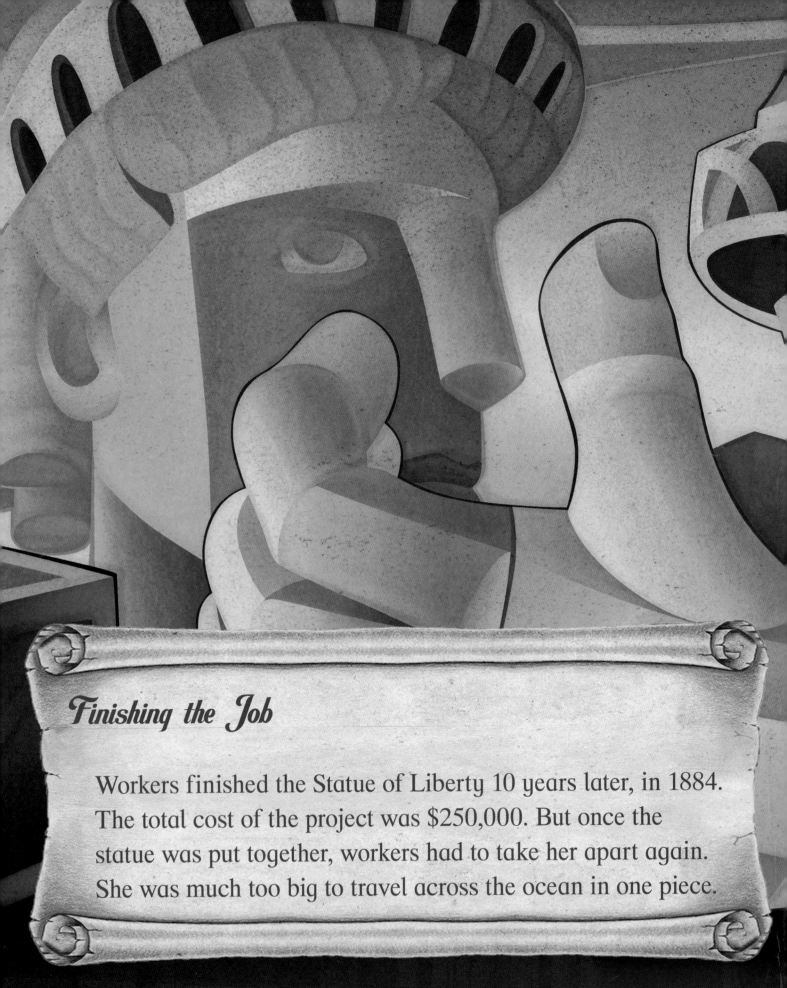

Finishing the Job

Workers finished the Statue of Liberty 10 years later, in 1884. The total cost of the project was $250,000. But once the statue was put together, workers had to take her apart again. She was much too big to travel across the ocean in one piece.

Her hands are 16.5 feet (5 m) long—about the length of a canoe!

Her index finger is 8 feet (2.4 m) long.

Her eyes are 2.5 feet (.75 m) across.

Her nose is 4.5 feet (1.4 m) long.

Her fingernails are 13 inches (33 centimeters) long and 10 inches (25 cm) wide—just a bit bigger than the book you are holding right now!

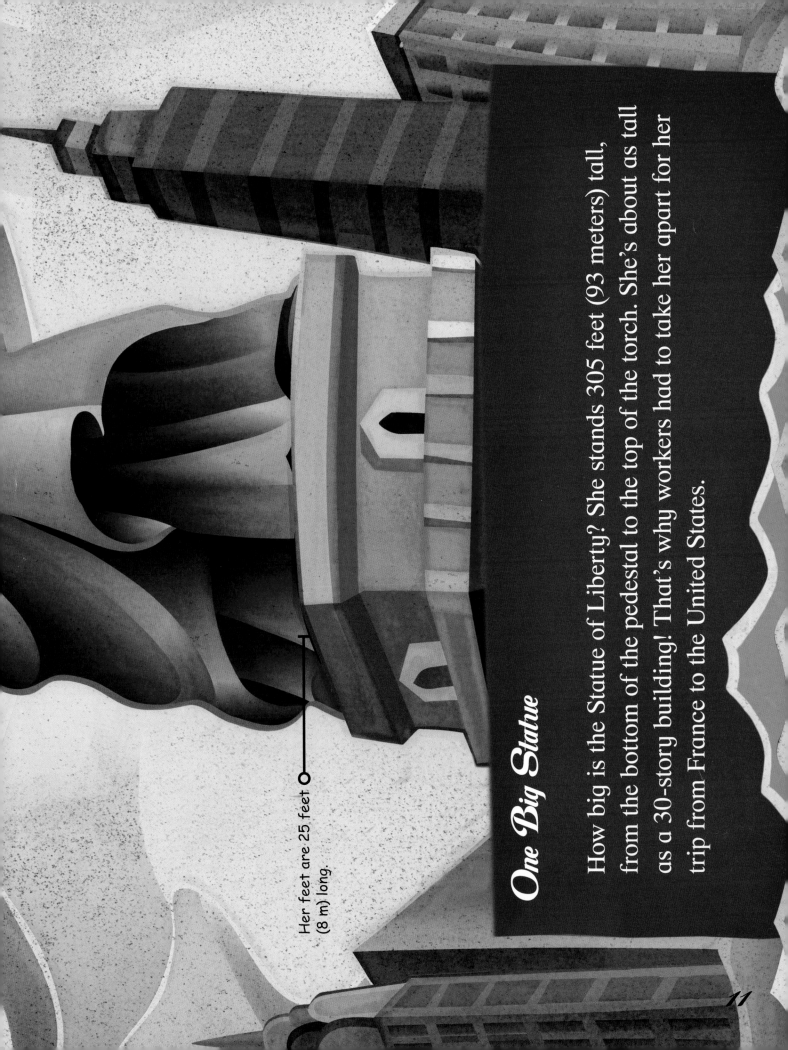

Her feet are 25 feet (8 m) long.

One Big Statue

How big is the Statue of Liberty? She stands 305 feet (93 meters) tall, from the bottom of the pedestal to the top of the torch. She's about as tall as a 30-story building! That's why workers had to take her apart for her trip from France to the United States.

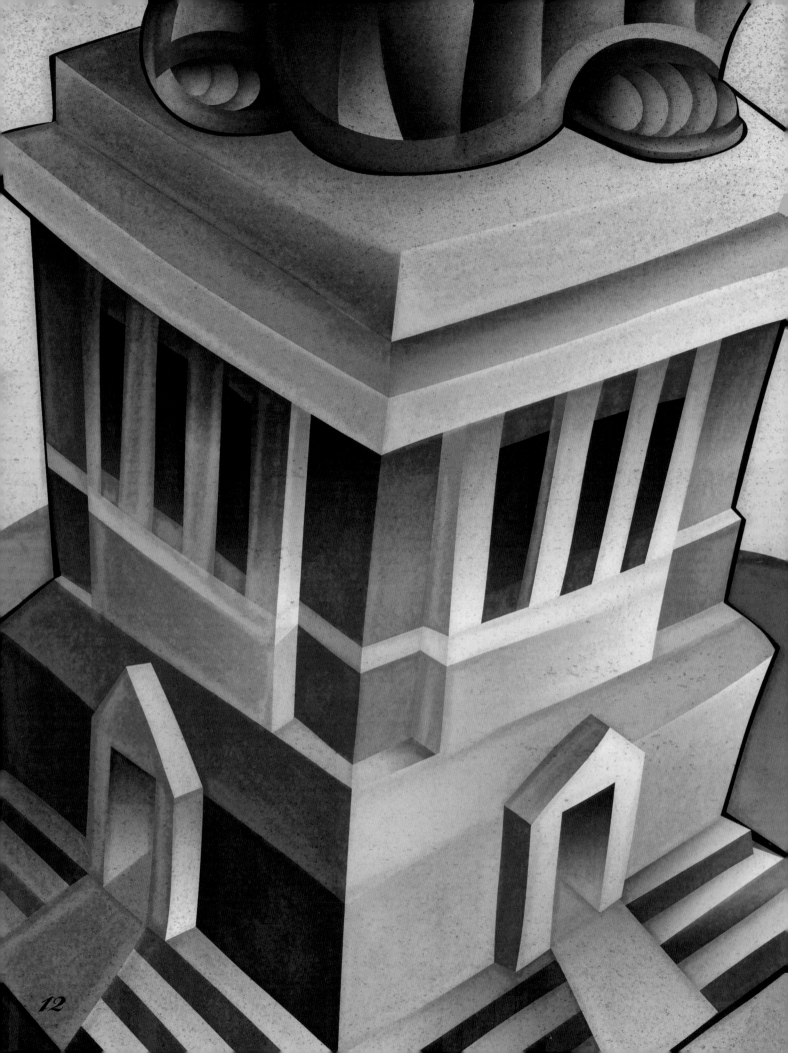

12

The Pedestal

French workers built the Statue of Liberty, but U.S. workers built her pedestal. She needed a base to keep her steady in bad weather.

Building the pedestal was going to cost a lot of money. Thankfully, a newspaperman named Joseph Pulitzer helped raise the needed funds. People from all over the United States gave whatever money they could to help the pedestal project.

Pulitzer collected about $100,000 for the pedestal project.

The Statue Arrives

Packed in boxes, the Statue of Liberty sailed into New York Harbor in June 1885. Her pedestal was finished in April 1886. Workers then spent four months putting her back together.

On October 28, 1886, President Grover Cleveland officially accepted the Statue of Liberty. Thousands of Americans were there to celebrate France's gift.

The Statue of Liberty was packed in 214 different wooden boxes, or crates, for her trip from France to the United States.

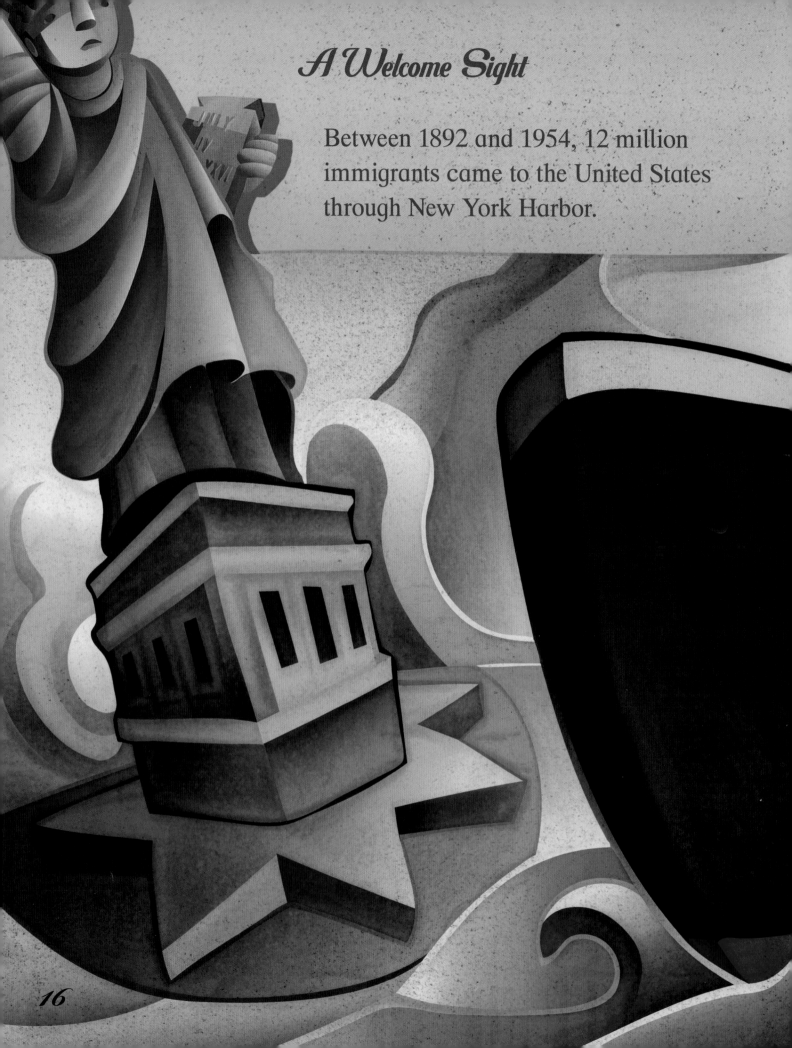

A Welcome Sight

Between 1892 and 1954, 12 million immigrants came to the United States through New York Harbor.

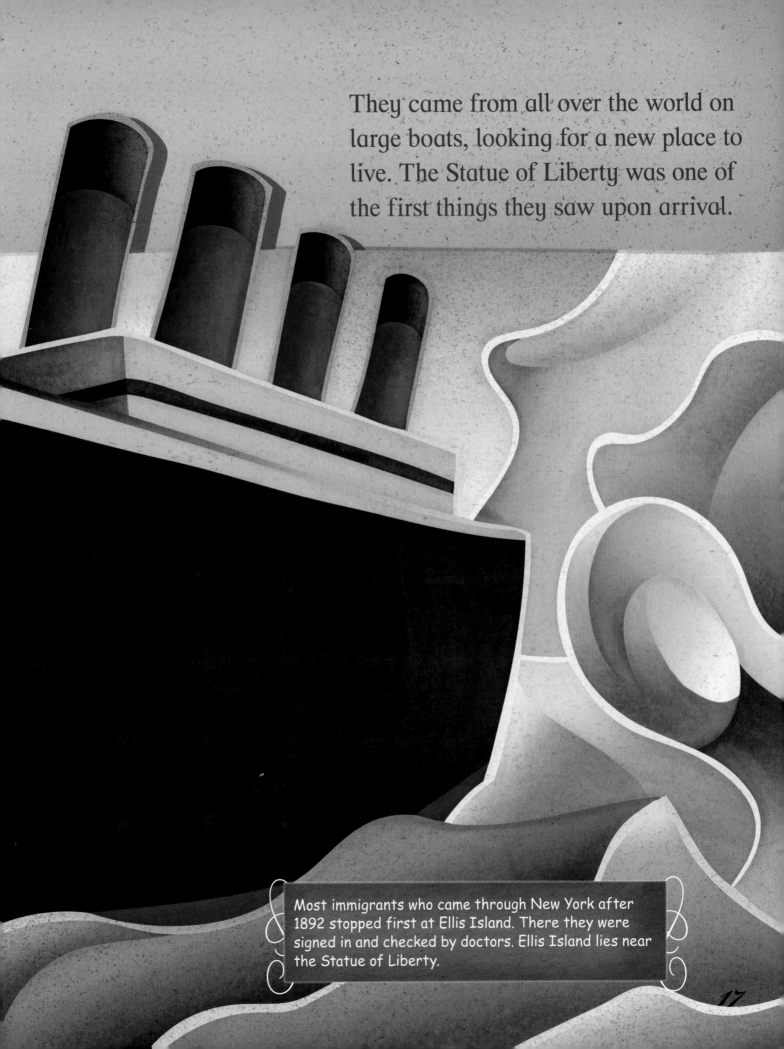

They came from all over the world on large boats, looking for a new place to live. The Statue of Liberty was one of the first things they saw upon arrival.

Most immigrants who came through New York after 1892 stopped first at Ellis Island. There they were signed in and checked by doctors. Ellis Island lies near the Statue of Liberty.

A Free Country

Many immigrants came from countries where they could not buy land. Most could not go to school. These rights and many others were only for the rich.

In the United States, almost anyone can own land and go to
school. The Statue of Liberty is a symbol of these freedoms.
She tells the world that the United States is a free country.

Liberty's Symbols

What do the Statue of Liberty's symbols stand for?

The burning torch stands for truth.

Liberty's crown has seven points. Each point stands for one of the world's seven oceans. It also stands for one of Earth's seven continents, or land masses.

The tablet is a symbol of the laws of the United States.

The date on the tablet, July 4, 1776, is a symbol of the day the Declaration of Independence was approved.

The broken chains, or shackles, that lie at Liberty's feet are a symbol of freedom.

JULY IV
MDCCLXXVI

The Statue of Liberty is much more than a pretty face. She stands for one of the United States' greatest gifts: freedom! Maybe you can come to New York City soon and visit us. We look forward to seeing you!

Statue of Liberty Facts

- The Statue of Liberty stands on Liberty Island in New York Harbor. Visitors can reach her only by ferry, a special kind of boat.

- It took nearly 30 years for the Statue of Liberty's copper to oxidize, or turn from reddish brown to green.

- There are 354 stairs from the bottom of the pedestal to the Statue of Liberty's crown.

- The poem "The New Colossus," by American poet Emma Lazarus, was inscribed at the base of the Statue of Liberty in 1903. It contains these now-famous words: "Give me your tired, your poor, / Your huddled masses yearning to breathe free, / The wretched refuse of your teeming shore. / Send these, the homeless, tempest-tost, to me, / I lift my lamp beside the golden door!"

Glossary

approved — given the OK

colonies — lands away from home that are controlled by the homeland, such as the American colonies of Great Britain

copper — a kind of metal

Declaration of Independence — the paper in which the American colonies said they were free from Great Britain

funds — money

immigrants — people who come to a new country to live

molds — forms that give something a special shape

pedestal — a base for something to stand on

Revolutionary War — (1775–1783) the Colonies' fight for freedom from Great Britain; the Colonies later became the United States of America

symbol — an object that stands for something else

re

Statue
...apolis:

. New
...huster
...ing, 2002.

...iberty!
, Straus &

Nobleman, Marc Tyler. *The Statue of Liberty*. Mankato, Minn.: Capstone Press, 2003.

On the Web

FactHound offers a safe, fun way to find Web sites related to topics in this book. All of the sites on FactHound have been researched by our staff.

1. Visit *www.facthound.com*

2. Type in this special code: 140482216X

3. Click on the FETCH IT button.

Your trusty FactHound will fetch the best sites for you!

Index

Look for all of the books in the American Symbols series:

The Great Seal of the United States
1-4048-2214-3
Our American Flag
1-4048-2212-7
Our National Anthem
1-4048-2215-1
The Statue of Liberty
1-4048-2216-X
The U.S. Constitution
1-4048-2643-2
The White House
1-4048-2217-8